JIMMIE MACGREGOR'S
SCOTLAND

Title spread photograph Bidean nam Bian, Glencoe

Jimmie Macgregor's
SCOTLAND

BBC BOOKS

By the same author

Published by BBC Books,
a division of BBC Enterprises Limited,
Woodlands, 80 Wood Lane, London W12 0TT

First Published 1993
© Jimmie Macgregor 1993
The moral right of the author has been asserted

ISBN 0 563 36816 0

Designed by Tim Higgins
Maps by Eugene Fleury
Photographs by David Ward

Set in Monotype Bell by Selwood Systems, Midsomer Norton
Printed and bound in Great Britain by Butler & Tanner Ltd, Frome
Jacket printed by Laurence Allen Ltd, Weston-super-Mare

Contents

The simplest of our games was the ring and run ploy, which had people jumping up and down answering doorbells. A touch of subtlety could be added to this by sending the most dough-headed of the group to ring the bells on the top landing, while the rest rang the bells at the bottom. With good timing the escaping dough-head would arrive on the ground floor in time to cop a skelp round the ear from an enraged ringee. A variation on the theme was achieved by tying together all the doorknobs on one landing, ringing the bells, and standing back to enjoy the ensuing tug of war. Simpler, but nastier, was the leaning dustbin. This was carefully balanced against the door. You rang and ran, and the victim opened up to a cascade of smelly garbage all over the lobby. We thought that was really terribly amusing. There was a consensus that the most satisfying games were those that most annoyed, frightened or disgusted people.

Not all of our diversions were irritating. Some were dangerous. The back courts of the tenements were a maze of railings, dykes, wash-houses and middens, and much of the time we spent ten or fifteen feet above the ground. There was great competition as to who could make the most impressive leaps between the rooftops. Distance was not the only criterion by which a jump was judged. A row of spiked railings between the two roofs added considerably to the jumper's reputation. All the railings in the back courts were fearsomely spiked, and the occasional injury, sometimes serious, was accepted as part of the hazards of tenement life. I have sometimes wondered about those spikes. Did the people who put them there see them perhaps as a deterrent to the disadvantaged hordes intent on breaking into the idyllic life of the tenements?

The girls had an extensive repertoire of skipping and ball games, with their accompanying songs and rhymes, while the boys played wee heidies, or keepie uppie, which consisted of heading a ball against a wall, sometimes hundreds of times. Everyone played street football, and the early training with the tannery ba' (sixpenny ball) is said to be the source of the *jinky* skills which once distinguished our Scottish footballers. Rounders was a popular game, which is why most Scots find the American fanaticism about baseball faintly daft. To us it's just rounders in funny hats. Cricket? No one had ever heard of it. There were also cissy round games like Bee Baw Babbity, which usually involved girls, and even kissing, and were normally played at school under duress.

Much more enjoyable were the confrontations with the kids from the Catholic school. We made faces, uttered what we thought were deadly swearie words, and hurled clods of earth at each other. Little damage was done, and both sides had a great time. No one knew why we fought the Catholics. It was sort of traditional. I didn't really know what a Catholic was, except that the Flynns were nice neighbours with odd pictures on their walls. Those ancient tribal rivalries have almost faded away, although there is a fanatic fringe that tries to keep them alive, but there was a time when an ill-considered answer to the question, 'Are you a pape or a prod?' could get you a rattle on the jaw. It was useless to try, 'I'm a Jew', for that simply brought the supplementary question, 'Aye, but are you a papish Jew or a proddy Jew?'

The Scots have accepted people of many races: Polish, Italian, Irish, Lithuanian, Asian, Chinese, African and West Indian, among others. This has been done with the minimum of friction, but perhaps we are still enjoying the remnants of our old prejudices too much to be bothered taking on any new ones. The nearest I've heard to a racist joke comes from the time of the trouble between India and Pakistan, when it was said that we had so many Pakistani lads working on the buses that there was a danger of the Indians bombing Parkhead garage. The orange and the green are just colours now to most sensible people, but in the 1950s an obstreperous wee drunk on the late night bus from George Square, on being told off by the Nigerian student conductor, retaliated by accusing him of being 'a big orange bastard'.

The life of the tenements ended quite suddenly. In the 1950s and 1960s there was an idealistic, but perhaps not too carefully considered, campaign of slum clearance, as it was called. Great areas of old buildings were razed, and the people decanted into the high-rise housing complexes which have proved to be such a social disaster. The whole project was well-intentioned, but based on modernist architectural theories developed on the continent, and inadequately adapted to Glasgow, with its less comfortable climate and different light. The process of change took place in a startlingly short space of time, and when the old tenement environment disappeared, it scattered long-established communities which never had the chance to re-group. The single-ends, the *Jenny a' things*, the *peeries*, the *bogies*, the *girds* and *cleeks* and the coal-fired black grates are now in museums visited by people still young enough to remember them as part of their everyday lives. The surviving tenements have now been sand-blasted back to their original rich russet, yellow, cream and honey colours. They are refurbished, modernised, much valued, and occupied by quite a different kind of person.

As the songs, riddles and rhymes of the streets were later to lead me to the

17

man called Stan Wood. He is jocularly known as Stan Stan the fossil man, but he is a serious and brilliantly innovative scientist, the more so for being self-taught. Once an insurance salesman, he now has his name appended to a fossil tree, discovered the oldest fossil reptile in the world, and proved that sharks once swam in the Glasgow suburbs. Stan is one of the few people who is capable of demonstrating in layman's terms the concept of a vast timescale, huge turmoil and movement, successive ice ages and hot spells, the gigantic power of the glaciers which gouged out places like Loch Lomond, and the great land masses moving around the surface of the globe. Scotland has some of the oldest rock in the world. The gneiss found on the island of Lewis and around the west coast is estimated to be 2500 million years old, and was thrust to the surface before there was any animal or plant life.

The Scottish landscape as we now know it began to develop only after the last ice receded. In time the barren wastes began to support hardy, ground-hugging plants like the lichens and mosses. These were followed by stunted scrub birch, alder and willow, which slowly but surely built up the soil structure, aided by the erosion of the softer rocks. Thousands of years were to pass before the development of real forests, oak and birch in the south and pine in the north, but several thousand years before the birth of Christ we had vast areas covered in Scots pine, with a mixture of rowan, birch, alder and other species. Long before Scotland was absorbed by England, many of our native wild creatures had vanished; the reindeer, the wild horse and the ox, while the bear and the beaver, the wild boar and the elk had disappeared from the diminishing woods. The crafty wolf managed to survive into the eighteenth century, but all was changing, and the great Caledonian forest itself was doomed.

Nature wrought the first great alterations in the landscape, but man continued the process. There are traces of humans here about 13 000 years ago, but they probably had little effect, as they were nomadic hunter-gatherers. The land really began to alter with the advent of farming, about 4000 BC. Trees were felled to clear ground for crops, and for implements and fuel. When man learned to build and to work metal, even more timber was required. Domestic animals sometimes enriched the ground, but sometimes laid it waste. As farming developed, burning and enclosing, ditching and draining began to change the face of Scotland, affecting every living thing. In our own time the pace of that change has accelerated beyond measure, and we are now capable of altering or obliterating in days, or even hours, systems which have taken centuries to develop.

The Typical Scot

A friend in Canada, who is a Cree, was once explaining the difference between the various tribes of the native Americans, and used the simple illustration that Indians of the wide open prairies tended to be tall and lean, while the canoe men of the west coast were short in the leg, with powerful chests and shoulders. I told him that if they had ever needed reinforcements on Vancouver Island, they should have come to Glasgow. Some people see that short, stocky Scot as typical, but on one occasion, while making a radio programme at the bull sales in Perth, I had to start selecting my interviewees carefully, because some of the farmers were so huge that my arm was tiring holding the microphone up. So who is the typical Scot? Is it the big-boned, broad-cheeked type from the Highlands and islands? Is the colouring blond or reddish, or is it

Mair's fish shop, Buckie

Dunvegan, Skye

PART II

DOWN SOUTH

Jim Mitchell, great-great-grandson of Tibbie Shiel

giraffe, these adoptive Scots graze contentedly around Bowerhope on the shores of St Mary's Loch. Llamas are attractive animals. They are doe-eyed and make a babyish bleating sound which is very appealing. They also tend to vomit on you if displeased. The Bowerhope llamas are in the care of Mandi and Derek Hook, whose two boys, Ronnie and Sam, were baptised in the old blanket-preaching ceremony. The blanket preachers were the hard-pressed Covenanters who, denied their churches, took to worshipping in the open air, often at great risk. The Hook baptisms took place on the other side of the loch at St Marie's kirk, bringing the total to three in a century. The old graveyard at the Kirk o' the Lowes has Catholic, Presbyterian and Episcopalian graves going back six hundred years. Many of the old memorials, like the remains of the original kirk, are now deeply buried, but there are still some very ancient stones and interesting inscriptions to be seen.

A Shepherd Poet

Most men will relish what is natural and simple if they are permitted to judge for themselves. If you take the most admired passages from the best authors, you will find them to be the natural expressions of men of good sense; and you will admire them, because you feel that they are precisely what you would have thought and said yourself on the same occasions; that they are, in fact, the things that have always been thought, but never so well expressed.

These are the words of James Hogg, known as the Ettrick Shepherd, and in his own locality as Jamie the Poeter; a man who rejected pretentiousness and strove for simplicity, yet delved, with the most acute perception, into the tortured complexities of the human psyche in his *Private Memoirs and Confessions of a Justified Sinner*. The work, long neglected, is now

Ettrick kirkyard

James Hogg, the Ettrick Shepherd

in the paths of literature', and observed: 'The walks of learning are occupied by a powerful aristocracy, who deem that province their particular right; else what would avail all their dear-bought collegiate honours and degrees.' He also realised that they would 'impede my progress by every means in their power'.

Energy, honesty and, most importantly, spontaneity, were crucial to Hogg in his writings, and he eschewed revision and editing. Like Burns, he has described his methods, and I am reminded of the oriental approach to painting, where the artist will make an intense study of the subject for days, weeks or months, and only when all the visual information has been absorbed will the accumulated knowledge be expressed in a minimum of swift strokes. 'Let the piece be what length it will, I compose and correct it wholly in my mind or on a slate, ere ever I put pen to paper; and then I write it down as fast as the A.B.C.' James Hogg had his first work published at the age of twenty-three, and by the time he went to Edinburgh at thirty-nine, he had a mass of successful writing behind him. Hogg remained his own man. He refused a knighthood, married Margaret Phillips and continued to live in his beloved Ettrick, where he combined his writing with farming, and where he continued to be known as 'Jamie the Poeter' by the people and in the places which had been his inspiration. During the Victorian era, his rustic background and absence of pretence and hypocrisy resulted in his works being consigned to oblivion by literary élitism and snobbery. It was André Gide who began the revival of interest in his work, with the recognition of the genius of *Confessions of a Justified Sinner.* James Hogg died in 1835. He is buried in Ettrick kirkyard, and his handsome monument looks over the loch to Tibbie Shiel's, where he spent so many hours in good companionship.

and Gartocharn. Just about every known British duck except some of the sea ducks can be seen here in the winter, together with whooper and occasional Bewick's swans. Wintering geese use the marshes in considerable numbers and there is always a selection of waders, some of which, like the redshank, find nesting sites here. Needless to say, this abundance attracts the predators, and hen harrier, peregrine and short-eared owl are sometimes joined by that flashy pocket Hercules among falcons, the merlin. Ospreys, now re-established in Scotland, are regularly seen in spring and autumn, *en route* to their nesting sites or feeding up for their migratory flights to the Gambia. The big fish-hawk used to nest on Loch Lomond, as it did on almost every decent stretch of water in Scotland at one time, and there are hopes that, if disturbance and misuse of the loch can be controlled, it may once again make its home here. The marsh also attracts greater rarities, and a spoonbill settled quite comfortably on the loch for a while.

As the osprey and pine marten were once widespread before being hunted to extinction in Scotland, so the wild boar and the wolf roamed around the loch at one time. They are gone for good, but the beautiful though rapacious marten will almost certainly reappear, so rapidly is it spreading in Scotland. This will be bad news for the grey squirrels, which have replaced the smaller and more attractive red species. Old ladies in parks look on grey squirrels as little furry friends: pine martens look on them as lunch. A new species already established in the area is the mink, a versatile and voracious predator whose rapidly expanding population derives from escapees from mink farms. Others were released into the wild by misguided supporters of animal rights. Some animal rights: certainly not those of the waterfowl and fish, small mammals and birds decimated by the object of their sentimentality. Mink will undoubtedly be an increasing problem, but at present there is a healthy population of mammals, ranging from the pygmy, common and water shrews, up through mice and rats, bats and hedgehogs, to stoats and weasels, rabbits, hares, foxes and badgers, to the largest of the animals, the deer. The red deer is our largest Scottish wild animal, and the smallest, the roe, is steadily increasing its numbers with the spread of forestry. The incoming sika deer are said to be inter-breeding with the red species, which could create a problem for the sporting fraternity. The sika is still very much a forest animal, and changes in the favoured habitats of the hybrid offspring could ultimately interfere with the traditional hill stalk. Even more exotic than the sika are the beautiful fallow deer, more associated with

Loch Lomond with the Inversnaid Hotel and Ben Lomond

gracious English parkland than the rugged landscapes of Scotland, and descended from herds established for the hunt on Inchmurrin and Inchlonaig.

The elusive otter is said to make use of the streams running into the loch, and the even more secretive and magnificent wild cat is well-established. Long-term residents, too, are Loch Lomond's wild goats, which are said to have lived here since at least the time of Robert the Bruce. There is a story that as the Bruce was fleeing (The Bruce fleeing? – never!) from the McDougalls of Lorne after an encounter at Dall-righ (King's Field), he shared a cave with some of the goats and accorded them the royal protection for all time. Gratitude indeed, for sharing a cave with goats is not everyone's notion of gracious living. Billy goats are not the most fragrant of creatures, though to be fair, their malodorous pong is apparently irresistible to lady goats. At a time when chlorophyll (the chemical which gives plants their green colour) was being promoted as a wonder deodorant, there was a rhyme which said:

> *The goat that reeks on yonder hill,*
> *Has browsed all day on chlorophyll.*

The Loch Lomond area is a plant lover's paradise, and Dr Agnes Walker, curator of botany at Glasgow's Kelvingrove Museum, told me when we visited the loch together that a quarter of the known British flora is to be found here. However, the most interesting life is probably to be found in the loch itself. There is a tremendous range and abundance of plants and small animals, supporting the larger creatures. The bulk of the plant life is found around the shore and where the light can penetrate to the bottom, but the upper layer of the water is rich in microscopic algae and plankton. This, together with the invertebrates, provides food for the several species of fish which flourish in the loch. These include eels (sometimes very large), salmon, sea trout, roach, perch and several others, which attract visiting ospreys and the normally sea-fishing cormorant. There are some oddities, too, like the powan, a sort of freshwater herring, found only here and in Loch Eck, near Dunoon. The powan is very rarely caught by anglers as it feeds on the microscopic plankton. Strangely, its cousin in Loch Eck is a bottom feeder, and shares its territory with another rarity, the Arctic charr. The Loch Lomond powan has been here for a very long time, but a much more recent arrival, first noticed in the loch in 1982, is the ruffe, which has an unfortunate taste for powans' eggs. Loch Lomond supplies water to Glasgow, and in 1982 the ruffe represented 8 per cent of the fish trapped in the filter screens. Three years later, 76 per cent of the fish in the screens were ruffe. Some introduced fish are escaped live bait, normally used by pike fishermen; others are brought in to improve the sport. A thousand years after the Ice Age, Scotland had about twelve species of fish. After another thousand years, only five more had appeared, but in the last 180 years no less than fifteen new species have arrived, all or most introduced artificially, with results which are not yet fully understood.

I am unaware of the number of fish species, if any, which have been introduced by the Loch Lomond Angling Association, but they have certainly added a number of entertaining, and in the main rather unlikely, fish stories to the mythology of angling. I heard a great number of them on a long, wakeful and, it must be said, very jolly overnight stop at the Inversnaid hotel, during the making of my radio series on the West Highland Way. My favourite concerns a group of elderly anglers who embarked on some night-fishing after having partaken of several small refreshments in the hotel. The euphemism, 'a small refreshment' is one much used in the west of Scotland and may require some explanation by example. The wee man gyrating around the late night bus stop, shouting at innocent passers-by, 'Is it a song yiz are wantin'?' may be said to have had a small refreshment. The same would apply to the inflamed sixty-five-year-old who is challenging four navvies to a 'square go'; and the guest who is found the afternoon after the party, in a comatose condition, with his face in the sherry trifle and one leg up the chimney, has simply been enjoying a small refreshment. It appears that one of our anglers was so refreshed that he contrived to drop his false teeth into a very deep dark Loch Lomond. There was great weeping and wailing and gnashing of gums, until a waggish member of the party, who had surreptitiously lowered his own wallies over the side, reeled them in with cries of triumph and jubilation. The toothless one removed them from the line, tried them for size, commented, 'Naw, they're no' mine', and threw them back into the water.

The road on the eastern shore of the loch peters out at the Rowardennan hotel, and to reach the Inversnaid hotel further north, it is necessary to hoof it along the rugged track of the West Highland Way, or to drive the roundabout route from Aberfoyle. Inversnaid, standing as it does on the loch shore, at the only natural break in the surrounding hills and at the end of the road into the Trossachs, has always been strategically important, and a natural stopping place for those on the great highland tour. Manley Hopkins paid tribute to the wild grandeur of the place and made an early conservation plea in his words,

> *What would the world be, once bereft*
> *Of wet and wildness? Let them be left,*
> *O let them be left, wildness and wet;*
> *Long live the weeds and the wilderness yet.*

It was here, too, that William Wordsworth penned his tribute to the 'Sweet Highland Girl'. I remember that I had to learn the poem at school and I thought it was a load of sentimental old codswallop, but when I was researching for a television series in the area, I made a point of re-reading the poem. I thought it was a load of sentimental old codswallop.

There are hotels at Balloch, on the extreme south end of the loch, and as one goes up the west shore there is Luss, Inverbeg, Tarbet, Ardlui and Inverarnan.

Tom Weir, Scotland's best-known outdoor man

abhorrent. Others feel that the park idea has not been properly thought through. The operation of national parks varies considerably in countries where they do exist. If the Windermere boaters do come to Loch Lomond, what do we do with them? Like the water skiers they have to be considered, and if we throw them off, are they simply being moved on to become someone else's problem? National parks probably need to be incorporated in some kind of overall national countryside policy for Scotland, and not used simply to protect specially chosen areas. Whatever the answer is, it has to be found and acted upon rather quickly.

Children of the Mist

Gregor Macgregor of Clan Gregor, first cousin to the great Rob Roy, was the last clan chief to be buried in the ancient ground of Inchcailloch with all the traditional grandeur of ceremony accorded a highland chieftain. His death was also to elevate Rob Roy Macgregor indirectly to the position of chief of the Gregarach. After several nights of the customary wake, Gregor's body was loaded on to a galley flying a black flag, and accompanied by boat-loads of mourners. As was the custom, the funeral galley three times described a circle on the waters, following the direction of the sun, then to the

The old burial ground, Inchcailloch

months, the chief decided to surrender himself and his immediate kinsmen to MacCailean Mor, who had prompted him in the Glen Fruin raid. MacCailein Mor's promise that they would be given safe conduct to England was false, and Macgregor and five others were publicly hanged at Edinburgh's Mercat Cross in January 1604. Others were hanged or beheaded later, and Glenstrae's family was virtually wiped out. Before his death, Macgregor recorded his betrayal by Campbell of Argyll, and detailed how Argyll had used the Macgregors against his personal enemies. The clan fury was white-hot and there was a period of ferocious reprisal against all whom they perceived to be their enemies, but things were changing. The crowns were united in 1603 and James could not wait to get to London. The eyes of the powerful in Scotland were also turned to the south, and for a time attention was diverted from Clan Gregor.

Kilchurn Castle, Loch Awe

The clansmen were now without a chief, living on their wits, and taking a variety of names, including the ancient one of McAlpin. The proscriptions against them were renewed and extended over a period of years, although their fortunes took an upward turn as a consequence of their support for King Charles in the civil war of 1638. The main reason that they supported Charles was that the Covenanters were led by a Campbell. When King Charles was restored and Argyll executed, the Macgregors had hopes that their old territories would be restored to them. As soon as the King was plonked down in the big chair, however, his interest in Scotland and the Macgregors began to fade, and the opportunist royalist Campbell of Glenorchy, among others, contrived that from here on the Macgregors would be landless.

Highland Rogue

Rob Roy Macgregor is undoubtedly one of the great Scottish folk heroes. Everyone knows of him, even if they know little about him. He is sometimes referred to as the Scottish Robin Hood, but not by Scots, who tend to think of Robin Hood as the English Rob Roy. No one knows for certain whether a Robin Hood ever existed except in legend, though someone like him probably did, but Rob Roy was very much flesh and blood, and his life and exploits are well recorded. He was deeply involved in the affairs of his time and was familiar not only to the ordinary people of the highland glens, but also to the great and powerful of the land. So well known was he, indeed, that when he was outlawed it was not even thought necessary to put his likeness on the wanted posters. Rob Roy is an English version of the Gaelic Rab Ruadh, which means Robert the Red, and refers to his violently coloured hair and beard, yet although his appearance was well known and clearly remembered long after his death, no likeness was ever made of him in life. On the wall of my lounge I have a double life-size head and shoulders of Rob, taken from a woodcut in Kenneth MacLeay's famous biography of 1818. It is from the only known painting of Macgregor, and drawn from memory and description. There is a good copy of the painting in the Helensburgh library, and the original is in Buchanan Castle, near Drymen.

incident as much as anyone else. The second incident took place toward the end of Rob's active life, and had more serious implications. A dispute over land had arrived at the stage of armed confrontation and, wishing to avoid a bloody battle involving several hundred men, Macgregor gave way on the question of territory, but to satisfy his and his clan's honour, offered himself in combat. His opponent, Alasdair Stewart of Appin, was an able swordsman of half Macgregor's age, and honour was satisfied when he cut Rob's arm. Macgregor gave best and congratulated the young man on being the only opponent who had ever drawn blood against him. Stewart was equally gracious in victory, acknowledging that only his youth had won the day. Rob Roy saw that the years had indeed taken their toll, and never drew his sword again.

When Rob Roy Macgregor became their chief, the Macgregors found themselves at last with a leader who not only embodied all the traditional qualities of head of the clan – honour, pride, loyalty and courage – but more importantly, displayed an agility and subtlety of intellect which was more than a match for the devious double-dealing and treachery of the powerful enemies who had encroached so far on Macgregor lands and rights. So much admired and respected was he that the great and greedy began to see that it was better to have him as a friend than as an enemy, and at various times he was much favoured by Campbell of Argyll and by the Duke of Montrose. The latter was to be friend, mentor, and ultimately the man who turned Rob Roy to full-blooded outlawry.

When Rob Roy married Helen Mary Macgregor of Comer, they lived on the north shore of Loch Katrine, but Rob was later granted land for a house at Inversnaid by his cousin Archibald, who was then clan chief, and had already seen great potential in the young Robert. He was also given holdings on the west flank of Ben Lomond, and the area known as Craigroyston on the east shore of the loch. About a mile north of Inversnaid, the cave which had been associated with Robert the Bruce four hundred years earlier was used by the Macgregors as a hiding and meeting place, and became known as Rob Roy's cave. Rob Roy's prison, in the same area, is a huge rock from which those offending against the Gregarach would be lowered on a rope to be doused in the loch. Confessions of wrongs or repayment of debts were usually achieved at the next stage, when the rope was moved from waist to neck. The little black highland cattle which were moved on the hoof in thousands to the trysts at Crieff and Falkirk were the mainstay of the highland economy. The attitude to the animals was ambivalent, and helping yourself through a little cattle lifting, or rustling, was accepted as the norm. The Macgregors, among others, set themselves up as 'protectors', delivering safe passage of stock through troublesome areas. Needless to say, the whole thing operated on the sharp stick principle. 'If you pay some money, you won't be poked up the nose with a sharp stick.' 'Who do I pay?' 'Me.' 'And who is going to poke me up the nose with a sharp stick?' 'Me!' Rob Roy was one of the most reliable protectors, conducting himself honourably, albeit within the rather flexible mores of the time.

Rob Roy Macgregor's grave, Balquhiddar

Simon Bolivar, who was raising the country in revolt against the rule of the Spanish. The only thing Macgregor seemed to enjoy more than poking his nose into other people's business was a good fight. There were plenty of them, and despite the disadvantages of a horrendous climate, unfamiliar terrain, and no knowledge of either the language or the local politics, Macgregor threw himself whole-heartedly into the business in hand. He was tough, resourceful and a natural leader, and piled up success on success. In no time at all he was weighed down with medals and honours and was supreme general of the army. Simon Bolivar was jolly pleased, showering Macgregor with honours and, more importantly, introducing him to his niece, the notably scrumptious Donna Josepha. Gregor moved in swiftly, and the famed Celtic charisma swept the Donna off her feet, as the famed broadsword had swept many an unfortunate Spaniard off his.

There followed a string of incredible victories, on sea as well as on land, and among the South Americans Gregor enjoyed the same reputation as his famous clansman Rob Roy had done in Scotland so long before. As he was to prove, however, this Macgregor did not trouble himself with codes of honour and such trifles. When he landed on the mosquito coast in Nicaragua, he found himself in what had briefly been a British colony, some thirty years before. The climate and conditions had been intolerable, and those who had survived had sensibly moved on, but Macgregor found some doting old chief who happily signed the whole territory over to him. This is when he began to develop his little notion. When he returned to Britain, it was as His Serene Highness Gregor I, Prince of Poyais. On the journey over, Donna Josepha had turned into a princess. He presented himself with great style to King George IV at St James's Palace, where his grandfather had done his show with sword and axe for the king's grandfather. He even had a chargé d'affaires, who was described as a Commander of the Illustrious Order of the Green Cross, and a major in the regiment of horse guards. The idea of a regiment of horse guards in a jungle swamp is bizarre to say the least, but His Serene Highness and grand master of the fabulous fib was not only accepted, but welcomed with open arms.

Having got clean away with this bit of outrageous nonsense, Gregor started to print his own money. Literally as well as figuratively. The impressive Poyais notes incorporated the old clan motto of the Macgregors, *'S Rioghal mo Dhream*, and were accepted as readily as everything else. In the modern world people are outraged by brochures offering glamorous pictures of hotels which are only half-built when one arrives, but Macgregor had no trouble whatsoever in passing off handouts showing a fine city, where only disease-ridden wilderness existed. His natural boldness inflamed by these easy successes, he next persuaded the Lord Mayor of London to get his bank to make him a loan of the incredible sum of £200,000. By the time Gregor got to Edinburgh, his picture of a land of milk and honey was well-established as fact, and he set about selling non-existent acres and taking good Scots notes for his bits of Poyais paper. It is difficult to know whether Macgregor's ruthless exploitation of the gullible Edinburgh citizenry was a belated revenge for the vicious ill-treatment his forebears had received there, or whether he was simply flushed with the success of his deceptions and motivated by simple greed. Whatever the reasons, he had soon organised a shipload of fifty people to depart for the promised land, to be followed almost immediately by another hundred and fifty.

At this point, the story ceases to be amusing. The hopeful adventurers found themselves in a horrendously hostile environment, and disaster struck immediately. Before they had even landed all their equipment and belongings, there was a violent storm which destroyed their two ships. The settlers did their desperate best, but by the time the story of their plight was known and help had been sent, the majority were dead. The colonial agent of British Honduras sent an outraged account of the disaster to Britain, but with the aplomb of the true con-man, Macgregor responded with a dismissive and quite witty letter to *The Times*. Once again, he came through unscathed. In France, he surpassed himself, raising no less than £300,000 this time, and sent a shipload of French hopefuls on the same incredible journey that had had such disastrous results three years before. This time, on his return to London His Serene Highness landed in the nick, but characteristically talked himself out again. When his money ran out, he simply contacted the government of Venezuela. They really did owe him something, and he was taken back and given a pension which sustained him quite comfortably as a Venezuelan citizen until his death. Apart from a very short term in prison, he got away with all of it, made a lot of money, fools of the Scottish and English establishment, and a hero of himself, at least to the people of South America. His portrait is on display in the National Portrait Gallery of Scotland in Edinburgh.